Motherland

Meg Knight

Presentation by *BookLeaf Publishing*

Web: www.bookleafpub.com

E-mail: info@bookleafpub.com

ISBN: 9789358313000

First edition 2024

This book is dedicated to my mother, Alexandra, for being both my anchor and my wings. There are no words to describe what you mean to me.

And to her mother, Annie, for always being there. I can't wait to meet you.

Motherland

You are clung onto a board,

In the middle of a vast ocean.

The sky above is storms,

With pockets of peace that will never be yours.

And you're grateful,

For the ship that sank and left you here.

And you're grateful,

For the black sea that you float upon.

And you're grateful,

For the sky's endless storms,

And for the brief and shattered moments,

That they smile down upon you.

"Fuck", you'll exclaim, "I was on a *boat*!

Not everyone has been on a boat!

And I was really *on* it, *in* it, *was* it!

And isn't it *beautiful*,

This endless black ocean?

And aren't I so *lucky*,

To be so close yet still not drowning underneath?

Keep your pity please because actually,

I feel fucking *blessed*!

To have witnessed what the *sky* can do,

What *storms* are for,

And I've been *drenched* and *scorched* and now,

I'm on a *board*! *This* board!

Who could have thought?

Not everybody *has* a board!

Isn't life *beautiful*?

Aren't grief and love the same?"

And you'll live every moment,

Riding each wave.

You know that one day you'll be beneath them,

With the ships and the stories.

Every day I am so grateful for you,

Every second I'm in awe.

But some days I quietly pray,

That I don't find myself clung to that board,

In that vast endless ocean.

I say that with shame,

Because I don't pity or blame,

And I don't want you to be ashamed,

It's just - I wouldn't be so brave.

To take so much pain and give back only love,

And be *grateful*.

I'd be happy just to be half of you.

And if some days you could scooch,

And if there was room for two,

On that board, in that vast open ocean.

I would swim out to you, clamber up,

Hold you with love,

For as long as the moment allowed.

And while you sit adrift,

I would steer and chat shit,

Through the storms and the sea to an island.

You could plant and root,

Soil soft underfoot and give way,

To the growth that begins in this ground.

Safe in the knowledge that I am here,

You finally exhale.

Losing sight and feet,

Become leaves and trees,

Without fear you return to the earth.

I will water the soil.

I will hold back the ocean.

I will shelter the storms.

We will call this land Mother,

This is our Motherland.

Let your children lead you here.

Let me look after you.

Let roles reverse in ways you never got to.

Let your mum live within this love.

Let history rewrite itself.

If you must, trust nothing else,

But knowing that you will be held,

By me.

And grow old, safe and loved.

This is what I want for us.

Wherever that board you are clung on to ends

up,

You are never too far from my love.

Child

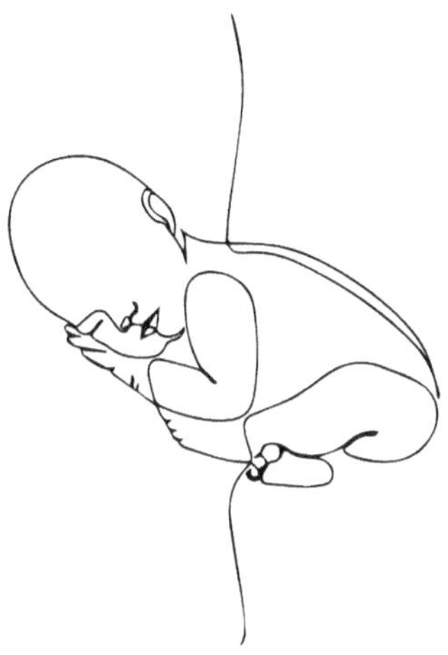

Today I feel like a child craving for a home,

The step we sat upon to watch the sunset,

The room we painted orange so that the sunset

never left.

Sometimes I am a mosaic. Sometimes I am a

puddle.

Endless bags of flour forming mountains on the

floor,

Always I am trying to fly, practising my form.

Always I am in the wars, bathing scars in warm
water,
Peeling back tights stuck to pus that had dried,
Become scabs over wounds that I'd hastened to
hide.

I want to ask the world if there will be a love
that stays?
I wish that we had more days in the room we
painted orange.
I somehow knew, even then, that colour meant
freedom,
The likes of which I've not known since.

Each time the sun sets, I'm six.
Clinging on, orange paint-stained fingernails,
Dreams torn like wallpaper ripped from the
walls,
Begging you to stay.

These walls, the first taste of safety,
This sunset-coloured womb where I once flew,
And I had you, all to myself.

Father

Something I still wonder -

Why you wanted to throw me at walls,

And teach her to climb trees?

Flying

I'm so small the chair is a mountain,
I push it centre stage,
Clamber onto the platform -
My flight deck.

I remember the launch,
The furious flapping,
The inevitable fall,
Never feeling defeated.

I dedicated time,
Got organised,
Practised every night,
I always knew that I could fly.
I'm still flying.

Every time I dream,
Every time I love,
Every time I lose,
I stayed furious.

I flew at you and fell,

Each time adding weight to my wings,

My growth will take me upward,

Skies cannot contain me.

Home

Do you remember the mosaic?
On the wall in the kitchen of the house,
Where we were happy.
Blue and white,
Dolphins and sea and freedom,
Our ongoing masterpiece,
A privilege to partake in.
I always wonder, yet never ask,
How close it came to being finished?

I was six years old when I found happiness,
And deep down I knew,
And clung on to and relished it.
Wisdom of old souls.
Digging in my heels,
I was peeled from that home.
But I learnt a better lesson,
That each break adds to the mosaic,
That things come apart to create.

Do you remember the promises we made to each
other?
About being all we needed?
We left it all unfinished.
In a parallel universe we're adding paste to
smashed ceramic,
Eating kiwis in an orange room,
Letting sunflowers loom.
The place my heart always returns to,
The first and last feeling of home.

Held

If you want to know how I am,

Hold my hand.

And I will cling to you like a newborn infant,

So tightly, utterly overwhelmed,

As if all life depends upon it,

An ancient and a primal grip.

Beyond belief, how strong.

How desperately we hold on.

Please return that urgency,

Make sure she feels it.

She grew up so fast,

And so rarely lets herself be held.

Monsters

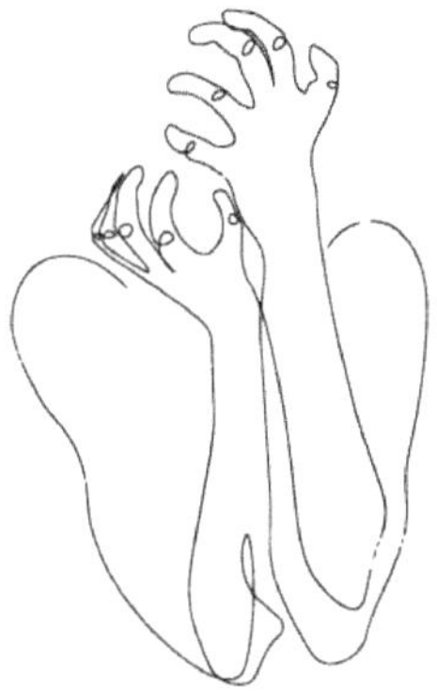

Sometimes,

You have given in to such monsters,

That home is no longer a safe place to be.

Only because,

The people there,

Want to keep you safe.

Ode to Cohen

I am at home,

When I'm alone with you.

Head resting on chest,

Breath is happy here.

A Thousand Kisses Deep,

My skin reeks of your influence.

Your wounds become cracks,

To pour my light into.

And it's your love,

Clamorous and proud,

Which roars louder than my demons.

Sea Meets Stone

I look for you,

Camouflaged in seas against skies split open.

Light pouring in,

Filling up the cup I kept empty for you.

As I watch you turn to rocks,

Too late,

I am already the sea.

I throw myself against you,

And break.

You are buried under horses' hooves.

How can they be wilder than me?

The End of Love

He drinks and paces,

Paces and drinks.

Sometimes a sound,

The one he makes when he loves,

The one he makes when he leaves,

Are the same.

The cliffs are tall,

And the church tower is taller,

She will wreck herself upon them.

The sunset spills across the sky,

Gives all it has, then leaves.

She is tired of the lies lovers tell to each other.

Tired of the dance that leads to the long walk,

That leads to the steep drop,

That leads to the end of love.

Stranded

Love breaks and rolls,

Like the sea against serpentine scars,

I summit the bluff and consider,

Slipping into the masterpiece,

Unlike my heart I can't trust my bones,

To shatter and survive. Shatter and survive,

Whilst I am on the cusp a man whose cup,

Runs over with easy promises,

Sits. Stable. Still.

I tether myself to the bight and welcome the

tide.

Survival Instinct

You are a long time falling apparently,

It feels like an eternity.

You make the decision immediately,

Not to leave.

You change your mind,

And the lucky ones survive.

But don't succeed.

Broken Birds

I keep seeing broken birds today.
Things that used to fly,
Laying stranded on the floor,
Crumpled up like torn paper,
Ghosts of our discarded dreams,
Absorbing brown puddle water,
Soaking into fractured wings,
Hopelessly confined to bent bodies,
Sky so close they can taste it,
Yet they'll never again be free.

Closure

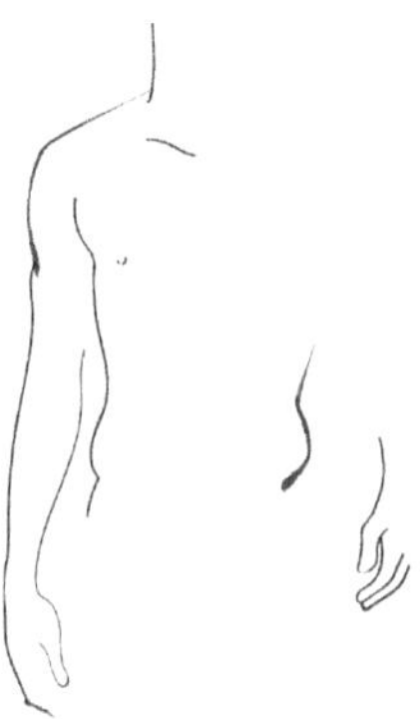

In getting complacent,

And hastening to replace them,

We talk about people as if they're not there,

Until they're not there anymore.

And it's a normal thing.

A defense mechanism.

To fill the cracks they left whilst leaving,

But still only being half gone.

And such powerful things are we,

With the same purposeful minds,

We fill in the cracks in space and time,
The ones that opened up to let their love in.

We pour thick concrete.

Wait for it to harden.

Call it closure.

Chicken Soup

The grief comes in waves.

I think of you when I make chicken soup,

And mourn at the loss of a comfort food.

The last compliment you gave -

You told me I looked fuckable.

I desperately devoured your crumbs,

Desperately blind to how thin I'd become.

Woken by the heat of bones burning on stove,

Thick-bottomed pan that once shone,

Rendered black and dull.

A shameful stain reminding us of our mistake,

As if to say- You will not get it right this time.

You said that I looked fuckable.

I wish that you had said-

How proud of me you were,

And how infinite your love for me was.

We Stay Alive for Each Other

I said,

Why don't we go outside, walk a while?

To myself, I said,

I cannot save this soul with a stroll.

I realise that Vitamin D and a fresh sea breeze,

Seem trivial in the solemn face of suicide, but,

I still pluck at the straws and last chances,

From the ongoing eternity.

I plan our route carefully,

Humbled by how carved out we have been,

And how resiliently,

We remained for each other, both of us,

Silently waiting for the other to say -

It's OK.

It's enough.

You can let go now.

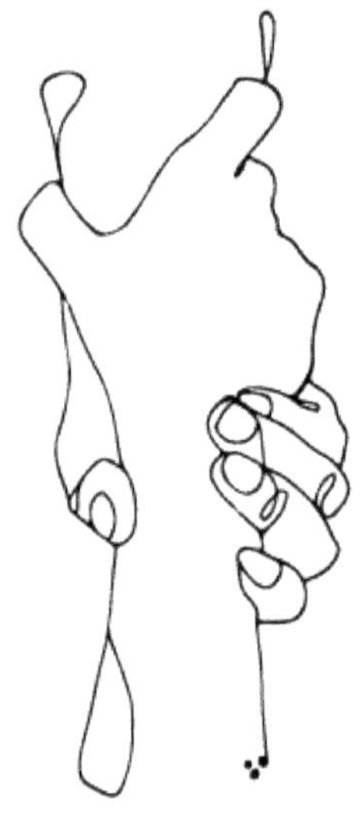

Lost Souls

He comes with pockets full of empty hands,
Fists holding broken promises,
And you tried to make a home in a house,
Where he can't spend the night.

She comes with the strength to build mountains,
Only knows how to dig holes,
And you tried to betray her with safety,
And explain all her crazy away.

The lost souls return to the sea,
Become storms.

How I Have Imagined This

A conversation flows between us,

My voice out loud as I greet you,

For the first time, feels like a stone.

Few words are spoken, tears erupt,

I open as a doorway.

I listen to myself elaborate on life,

And all my love for you.

Unable to move my gaze,

From the iris of your eyes,

Determined to make up for a lifetime.

I'm almost as old as you'll ever be.

I still remember the weight of you,

When you sat in my lap,

When you came to my dreams.

I know where you'll be waiting.

When my time comes, I'll meet you there.

It's Different Here

The vines that climb the trees are different,
How the trees offer skies their leaves is
different,
A breeze that feasts on my nervous system,
Eats away at my pain.

The way the mountains say my name is
different,
A call to be brave to those gentle to listen,
What if we showed parts of ourselves that we've
hidden?

Could we yet be held?
Could we yet be forgiven?
Perhaps here, we can.

The Visitor

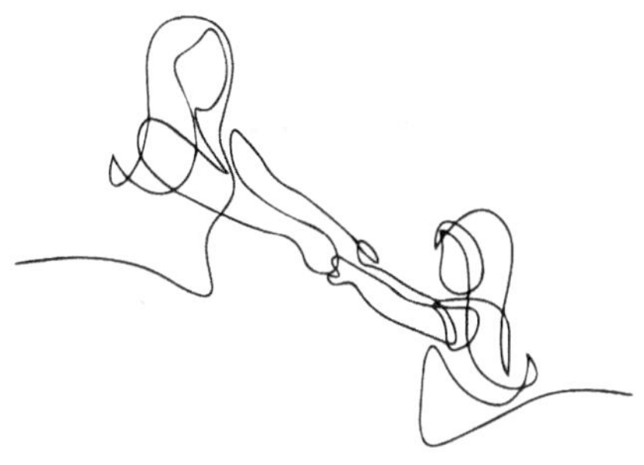

I long for a child to meet me in the kitchen,

To dance with me through madness,

To hold tightly and to whisper,

Hey. Listen.

I think she's here.

I think Joy's here.

Slipped in through the open window,

Sun spilling in,

Laughter leaking out,

She visits us so often now.

A Fence Post is Too Far

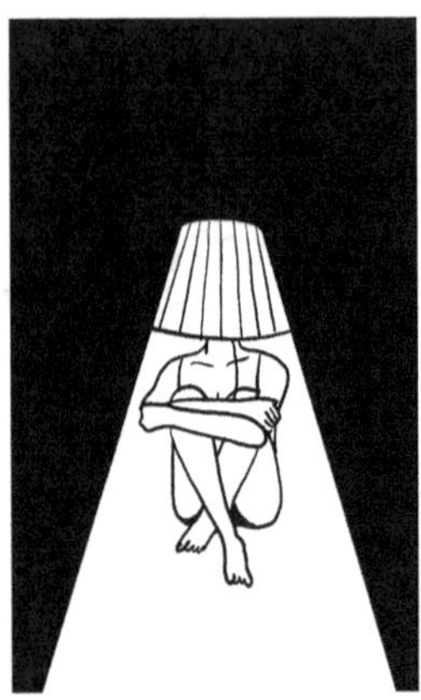

The crazy leaving my hair makes my heart ache.

Despite working so hard,

To come so far on this path,

Still I avoid the trap.

I'm unhealthily attached to a studio apartment.

Seems old ghosts live here still,

And thank God.

Baby ain't staying if the thrill is gone.

Standing in the shower,

I play with making time stop.

Wonder if I stayed here would it take them long?
To find old ghosts making homes under skin.

Don't go too far.
Some become sane,
And that is truly tragic.

Yours

Don't just live in this house,

Paint the walls.

Paint them with ideas,

Paint them with pain,

Paint them purple.

Build a fence,

Build a wall,

Dig a moat if you must -

Stop them from darkening your door.

If you cast your own home into shadow,

Let it be from the curtains you've drawn.

Undress and stand before a mirror naked,

Look at the house and the home you've created.

Let your thirties be about discovering,

A secret room behind a bookcase,

Wildflowers blooming into every unkept space,

Don't just live in these walls.

Let your home house your soul,

Let every door lead back to yourself,

Let every window be south-facing,

Hold yourself up,

Hold yourself on the floor,

Hold it and rock back and forth,

Find your way back here -

No matter what.

Find ways to love what is yours.

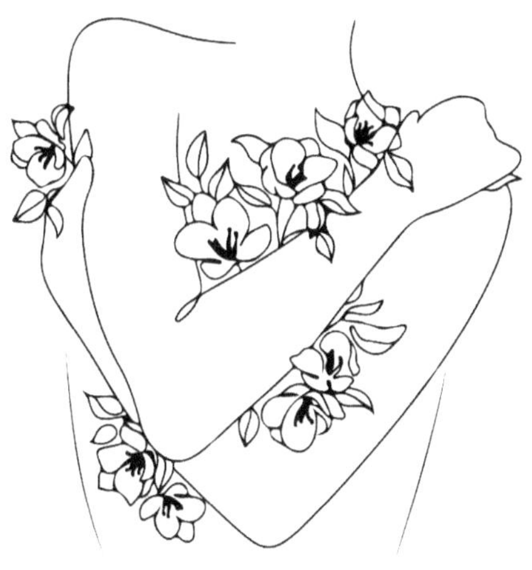

www.ingramcontent.com/pod-product-compliance
Lightning Source LLC
LaVergne TN
LVHW010938200726